Pepperm

Acknowledgements:*St. Peter's dog roses* appeared in*People's Poetry Letter*; *another ego* came to life in a different version in the anthology *Poems to Remember* (The Ontario Poetry Society, 2000).

Poet's Corner Award 2002 judges: Lorne Dufour and Jeanette Lynes
Cover photo © Janice Phillips, "Aurora Borealis #18". Reprinted by permission of the artist.
Design and in-house editing by the publisher, Joe Blades
Printed and bound in Canada
Simultaneously published as BJP eBook 35, ISBN 1-896647-84-7, Acrobat 3.0 PDF, with distribution via http://PublishingOnline.com

The Publisher gratefully acknowledges the support of the Canada Council for the Arts and the New Brunswick Culture and Sport Secretariat—Arts Development Branch.

Broken Jaw Press
Box 596 Stn A   **www.brokenjaw.com**
Fredericton NB E3B 5A6   tel / fax 506 454-5127
Canada   jblades@nbnet.nb.ca

National Library of Canada Cataloguing in Publication Data
Tessier, Vanna
        Peppermint night / Vanna Tessier.

Poems.
Also available in a PDF format.
ISBN 1-896647-83-9

        I. Title.

PS8589.E8284P46 2002   C811'.54   C2002-901976-1
PR9199.3.T436P46 2002

Peppermint Night

Vanna Tessier

Fredericton • Canada

To all eagle-eyed fighters who survived the unforgettable.

Peppermint Night

moonscar

petal of dusk
bruising the pledge of bare sky
your portrait cut out
black & blue freedom

gas-green tail chisels
the outline of a comet
haze of yellow dust
your shaggy hair
coiling around tomorrow's secret
streaking an El Greco shadow
a muffled promise of mist

train of light
trailing across the horizon
bluish i/ons of fear
motes silhouetting a frosty hood
a whisper to earth

a constellation's dare
flagging down
Sagittarius
        sharpening Cupid's arrow
its cue
incandescence
etched against our midnight

        a couple
        sketched in the dark
        seeking heaven

working things out

the girl in blue jeans
feeds the chickens grain
lets the piglets roll in the mud

it's only a matter of time before the rooster
crows three times
pointing a finger at you

raising eight children
all by herself

hot-blooded black-haired farmhand
spending her life   on the Prairies
where he leaves her   brokenhearted

washes bed sheets
knits scarves & sweaters
makes lacy bookmarks
bakes braided bread
blueberry muffins & cinnamon buns
for the whole congregation

        what more would you want?

in the high-steepled church
the preacher
blesses her
kneeling in a wooden brown pew
among ivory saints
& tanned madonnas

a row of saffron candles
their wicks   burning hot
skimming past tainted glass windows
on the other side of night

the faithful
know something
about grooming horses & milking cows
or making goat cheese

don't you worry
give her your palm to read

Jess can guess who you are
may tell you how to pray
& work things out

a private fight

a recruit at the military base
marches to the barracks
past the bull's eye

       learns to pull the trigger
       & strike a target right between the eyes

she runs the treadmill
the diet of the rat race gets to her
when two strong hands grab her
it's one of the muscular trainers
dragging her
inside a dim-lit warehouse

rain of punches
shoving her down
hitting hips/shoulders

      fight back!

she bites hard into his thigh
a private's mark

chain reaction   alienation
angst
reality sinking in

bloodshot eyes
raw rage
an ongoing struggle
all the way uphill
only to roll downhill

                    no respite
      for peacekeepers
                  locked in a private battle

pack a day

standing in line
i wait my turn to buy a newspaper
a means to be friendly
understanding people around me
a binding measure of sharing
the present   feelings

a man with a stubble on his chin
jumps ahead of me
charging at the cashier

here! a pack with menthol

he throws a $5 bill
on top of the counter

give me my pack

nods to the cashier who turns to him
i swallow hard placing two bits
on the glassy surface

for my paper

the cashier bows
& shoves the quarter
inside her metal drawer

what about my matches?

the man shoves back his cap
strands of black hair
stick out at the back of his head
spiders' legs crawling along his neck
he grabs his pack
rips the top off
shakes out a cig

> *what do you want with me?*
> *freaking me out, hah!*

he chews at the cig
a weapon dangling
from the corner of his mouth

i clench my teeth
don't want to know anything else
about this habit

i'm about to cross over the solid line
invading his s/pace
breaking down all barriers
to snatch away the cig
from his mouth

a cloud of smoke chokes me
damned!
i'll show him
what i can do
when i read my paper

a fruit fly

want to live
twice as long?

think of the fruit fly

fed mashed bananas
dates & brown molasses
to lengthen its life span
the insect will survive 60 days
while you'll double your payroll
as a lab technician

the next 500 generations
might thrive
living twice as long
on fresh fruit & spices

      vitamin "c"
      cantaloupe   honeydew melon
      figs   grapes
      sex overdrive/senses overload

what you need most
honey's vital taste & sustenance
sweetening your lifeline
rain   cooling you off
sorting out the harvest of centuries

the fruit fly
survives for you
giving you a hint of what you can expect
showing you the chance of keeping
time at bay
a family saga

shoving back conformity
the hands of a biological clock
aimed straight at you

whipping out a radical change
in your life span
mutation
genetics   DNA
a prohibited fruit

       falling
       from the garden of Eden

Sayuri

sold at age nine by her parents
to a Kyoto geisha house
a fisherman's daughter
leaves
her native village of Yoroido

will i ever see my friends again?

her older sister cries
on the train
they face a long ride
no bread no water
the unknown catches up to them
a stranger standing in front of a teahouse

big sister can't enter

the little girl with grey eyes grows up
in her role as a geisha
making men forget
who they are
away from their duties
their work

the present

better left alone among shadows
slipping
farther into the distance

Sayuri pours tea for a wealthy man
baring her pale wrist
pulls back her kimono sleeve a bit more
a glimpse of smooth skin

bare underarm
flashing a signal
flagging down
temptation

      a test of endurance
      the tea ritual
      breaks the ice
      between the two

touching
the sky-blue picture of her fan
tomorrow turns into desire
a landscape
living proof of virginity
worth more cash than you could ever have

      fingers trembling
      wiping tears
      from her creamy white make-up
      to see what's underneath
      another self

space

spring catches up
to you & me
restless buddies
needing more room
to call our own

we want to be closer
it's time
to clear the air
climbing onto cloud nine

orbiting the earth
misty visions
working out a new season
to carve a place

aboard the shuttle
we could shoot pictures
in different poses
naked bodies
on an interstellar panorama
looking for unity
a leap of faith
intimacy
a toast to life

an invitation
to share our spirits
with the stars

the Gardener

grabs a coil of sepia threads
roots wrenching sap
& minerals from the dirt
weathered fingers
twist a spruce tree branch
tracing leafy-green net
cornucopia of tints

lacy trellis filtering
an ochre-edged glow
coarse black hair
bony cheeks
darting olive eyes
watching curly vines grow

Gardener's arms weave a patch of sky
a swirling vortex of blue
filling the void in his heart

bends over the shoot of a sunflower
petals blooming
amber strokes
a rim of seeds
crowning a thick stem
long veined neck
carrying life juices

the vital rhythm
of the earth belting out its best

weeds choking the orchard
a silent thief
pair of hands/scissors
snatching away the quality
of the harvest

facing the robber of green growth
Gardener snaps ribs of leaves
violet dark veins
pulsating at his temples

re/action
a kaleidoscope of tinges
lilac nest
shades & hues
struggling
                for a breath of air

Gardener tends
tender plants
taking care of the verdant poplar
a tree of eternity must grow

he wipes off sweat & tears

                a rainbow
                arching over his garden

shogi

moves linking thoughts
for Yamamoto the player
who punches the 'go' shogi button
needing more speed
to crack the pattern
with a Zen-like posture
a God in disguise

no colour difference of the squares
on the 9x9 board
no shape of victory
for the pieces of opposite sides

no stalemates
in this chess computer game
only checkmates
            a king can't avoid the enemy
            escaping capture

his pawns can be redeployed
in a new strategy
to attack
their former master
            betrayal
becomes the all-eating monster
following
a different route
to swallow stone & shadows

in sheep's clothing

look through the stream of grains
racing down the neck of an hourglass
the colour of truth
texture of loneliness
slipping through your fingers
phantoms of another era still unfolding

no use for time
just a crumbling presence
transforming us
into what we don't want to be

carved in marble .& mud
a lone wolf
in sheep's skin
drinks in the tavern
gulping down sadness to forget
secret lies   delusions
distorting our day

tell us the story
without changing fate
a pilgrim searching
for what you have in mind

          the unknown
          dark side of midnight

the bake sale

almond scent spreading sweet news
the eggbeater keeping time with a rhyme
rhythm skimming cream off the top

she kneads dough for a feast
braiding the flavour of freedom
warming up the room
stream of familiarity/privacy
                    his arm stretches out
to touch her
still feeding hungry mouths
apple strudel/cherry turnovers

          the Bake Sale
          is on

she presses her lips tight

          bringing chocolate chip cookies
          pleasure a honeycomb
          sugar-coated crunch
          to share with friends
          what might be
          just another fortune cookie

the gingerbread boy grins
jumps off a lace-trimmed napkin
joins the lineup of muffins
diving headfirst into green tea
maze of leaves
floating

destiny
in your cup

a touch
of lime'd do you good

St. Peter's dog roses

bless the sinuous path to heaven
just a shot away
from here

long sleeves & no clam diggers allowed
in St. Peter's Basilica
where saints' eyes glow
greed an illusion
a shower of fireflies
shaping mind
sparkle of dust motes/myth
on a sand-smooth skull
glistening moon

a sermon
begging forgiveness
something we didn't do
the chisel hitting hard the knee of a still Moses

     "Act - now - re/act"
     the Maker/sculptor yells

you rush out   limping
Michelangelo crashing through the crowd
a streamer of dog roses
brushing against you
searching
for the meaning of summer embers

bats

project anger
raw rage
blowing you through the roof
mind carving a mission
for the survival of the fittest
a fallen angel saving face

bleak membrane vibrating sail
nasty flicker of grey
just what matters for a ransom
the measure of act/ions
getting out of hand

turning to radar
emergency flash/flesh
clinging to the edge of gloom
tips of wings quivering
in the black cave
everything becomes possible

night eyes peering out
blades piercing pores
a male flaps closer to a female
mate's hairy body
looming larger than life

rash of senses
blind segment of security
unwilling to let go of e/motions
the female is storing the sperm
sealed inside her body
until next spring
when she might pass the survival test
& get pregnant
on time   breathing tomorrow

love a message
in her heart
speeding up the pulse of destiny
spinning
faster than a pinwheel
taking off with flying colours

impression of relationship
a shadow filter
                crossing our path
safety   a touch
entangled in a nest of black hair

mysterious not/ions
keeping a close count
of what can be done
if you can't find an echo of truth

java

a fizzy streak
badge of honour
pointing to the frothy foam
bubbling over the rim of your mug
a soul-searching
concentrated effort to capture
all the flavour in the world
into a single drop

on the main counter many hands
a lineup of choices
propping up approval
for a loud burst of beans
an oath to get you anything
you want

      a shot of java
      liquid spring
      lovers' sighs

desire pushing you to go
where your heart wants to be
increasing your strength
      mapping your body
with ebony-blue veins
adding a tide of sugar
to savour life

she sips coffee
steaming hot
"Java"
still looking for him
alone

he stands out in the crowd
floating through the haze
aroma tempting buds
can't resist
her nod
an invitation to try out
something he never dreamed of

creamy dark richness
promise of a breakthrough
searching   for what
he might never find again
        over coffee

a script
sharing vision
bittersweet drink
swallowed fast
burning hot

who's raising the question
leading
        to more than a taste of java?

Head-Smashed-In

violet streaking fleece of clouds
cutting across the horizon
sharp knives
     horns poking storm
shaping lean notes
a shot of adrenaline
shoving you over the edge

a gleam of silver specks
on sandstone
     a faraway bison stampede
to Buffalo Jump
can't halt inevitability
when you reach Head-Smashed-In

baring teeth
biting into skull & bones
     hints from above
showing faithfulness
a burning glow for an ideal actuality

the proof we're seeking
about the past
threat to our identity
lost tinge of angst
unleashing anger/hunger
a rock personality drumming
driving buffaloes along stone boulders
framing death canyon
carved deep into a skeleton nightmare

wind gust eroding stone
an ice pick
jabbing troubleshooter

rotating weather vane
rooster cawing at the entrance of a cave
wetness
spraying the blessings of a waterfall

      walls perspiring
      rust

thick drops of blood
clinging tears
a deafening roar
blast from the wilderness
not for the faint of heart

another ego

violence
                spell inching closer to you
sliver of moon
cactus thorns poking into pores
                clinging to the other self

the image you want to project
a blur   delusion bleaching
relationship

change increasing strength
for a new trend
mystique braiding leaves
stealing the show
stirring sensations
for an alter ego
an unknown pattern of choices
shaping
your angel wings against the snow

a newcomer
straight poker-face
who knows how to play cards
better than you

makes you cry
when you lose your shirt

jamming

bass guitar staging a show
in a low key
promise to take on a tough role
the keyboard filling in for Calliope
a late night performance
recital for an invisible audience
a brain drill

popular tune
riding over the air waves
a date with the sax
sex frequency
breathing intimacy
a search for a plum reward

the guitarist kneels by the drums
doesn't belong here on earth
long ponytail sweeping shoulders
copper stubble
a shadow on his chin
each note   suspense
your choice
begging for more

      will work longer
      for a chance to see you

feeling blue tonight
         jamming
fate
      at your fingertips

escort

bent over his desk
he's still trying
to balance his figures
choice ruling
iron fist punching in numbers
notes on the keyboard
left for a stray mongrel
roaming alone among the Rockies

lets me rent a motel room
the flat-headed key in my hand
duty of a crescent moon
a good rest erasing trouble

had a big fight
didn't eat supper
would order fish & chips
but couldn't find a fast-food outlet open

    too late
    who's hungry?

    if you show up
    i'll get you a nightcap

never mind
all i need for now
is a meal escort
leading me to where
no one has ever eaten as much before

white-finned shark

the blade of a fin
cuts across
a rippled surface
lightning over a crop of waves
slicing through the path of peril

jet black jaws
jagged teeth   a menace
smack
under the belly of your boat
a warning bump
danger   too close to you

if you ever touch
the whitish scaly stomach of the shark
it feels rougher than fear
sandpaper skin
matching the bottom of the ocean

gnawing mandibles
chasing after an octopod
tentacles of apprehension
catching up to hunger
high tide
an unexpected ransom
terror & instinct
scrubbing your mind
                    blank

construction puzzle

torn denims
fluorescent orange vest/raincoat
amber helmet
blond tress swinging on her nape

she stands in the middle of the street
flags down motorists

musk promising enigma
changing puzzle   of possibilities

life checking you out for faults
headlights on
catching rainbow drizzle
a maze
shapes & colours
yielding means to another end

mind counting links
meeting with strangers

a green Chev slows down
swerves past a puddle
black rubber tires scraping hard
on wet gravel   roaring risk

a rockslide
catapult of the past
              all hell breaking loose
pouring mud
over the construction route

the girl lowers the crimson Stop sign
leans against a shovel

pulls down her helmet over her brow

      she doesn't want to face
      another real world
      & a traffic jam

not a chance

tough going for a trucker
driving his Ford half-ton
making it jump over mounds of rocks

he puts on his sunglasses
looking for what may be hidden
farther than anyone can see

his blind spot
doesn't send him a signal
as a violent gust of wind
blows stones
crashing against his windshield

a blast from limbo
clockwork splitting the image
of an aspen tree in two halves

secret energy
an air mass
moving too fast
to where you don't want to be

a cloud of dust & gravel
showering down unto the truck's cab
tree branches snap
shaking   the heck out
of the half ton

pain
sinking into flesh
for a trip with no return

your eyes take it all in

but who
tell me
who could get out alive?

fast food

a thin woman
widening her hazelnut eyes
watches
the sprinkling fountain of orange juice
beak filling up the tall glass to the brim
for a big gulp

> *it's like milking a cow*
> *at the farm*
> *just a moment*

she fumbles in her jeans pocket

> *can't find the change*
> *had the money right here*

think you can make it?
one day you will

she swallows hard
searching through her handbag

> *don't know what to do*

pushes her hair behind her ear

> *can you lend me something?*

i wave to her

> *sure can*

she smiles

    need a drink of pop
    & some french fries

i don't have to agree
she bends her head to one side

    need it fast

in this neck of the woods

to a Sardinian poet

never met someone like you
in my life
a Sardinian who could write
& speak like you do
in a language
i might not know
but remember
          on the other side of the ocean
we may understand each other
better in the woods

i'll learn the best & the worse
in a strange dialect
taste of salt
corduroy sand
showing
how rugged life is   on tall mountains
lush poplar trees   spindly oaks

cedars   green lattice of leaves
screening sun's rays
to ripen blackberries
onyx beads

a sieve filtering
the difference of customs
hot-blooded link
to where we might find
the meaning of shadow

an island standing   cragged
in the blue Mediterranean
murmuring siren

a confidential voice   private idiom
to those who want to explore
the rocky beach of life
stretching out arms
to fit the mood
soaking up moonlight
needling the stars

a drawbridge
past a ravine
the trestle of generations
shifting
to dig up
ribbed shells
murmuring things
only you can hear
among the nebulas
pulsating
ether & summer

raven's feathers blowing in sync
proof of existence
sliding
closer to your heart

anti-memoirs

to A. Malraux

hot air balloon sliding
over yellow cedar trees
to climb up to the mountain top
where a tea house
revolves on its axis
counting saw-toothed peaks
circling the valley

geologist grins
at the edge of the world

can't stand the pressure of life
crowding him in from all sides

solar flares bursting out
when he counts his blessings

energy level
increasing anguish

debating how to cope   with speed
on the fast slopes
identity piercing an ego
lost among lichens

pine cones sticking to the soles
resin scent
& notes set out
to find music

memoirs

something you can't forget
but wish you did at times

damp mosses
algae
leaving the rock stained
with souvenirs of pale hues
another era's growth

green & yellow leaves
unknown melodies
you wish to play some day

when you remember

Tarzan

leaps   to the present
metropolitan anachronism
bare-torsoed

burnt-out medical worker
escaping from his job   yesterday
stress hidden   behind the Roman grove
of leafy trees in the public park
surrounding Villa Borghese

used to bring back many
from comas   bloody hands
at accident scenes
until he lost it

                    had a near-death experience

now he plays his harmonica   to life
spontaneous re/enacting
                    outdoors
a taste of berries, mushrooms & hazelnuts

wild greens will give him
the power he needs to survive
taking the next breath of fresh air
when he jumps to the highest tree branch
a scientific conclusion

        a natural way of pumping iron
in patched trousers he climbs
        the next tree trunk
bandanna, trainers & green camouflage
he soldiers on for what it's worth

a cardboard box placed
near the statue of composer Gaetano Donizetti
is all he needs to discover
actual wisdom   reality
      & environment   in detail

they tell me he's looking around
the woods   still hanging
onto a lime vine
eyes on his future
        watching for a Jane

the pharmacist

dr Lee frowns behind the counter
a dried scorpion in a jar
& a flask of deer penis tonic
the best ingredients for your health

if that doesn't do the trick
try the small snake coiled
beside a potbellied bottle

hawthorn tea sealing a secret
the nourishing essence
can make you smarter
than you think

dr lets me   sit in his office
my wrist propped
on an orange beanbag

takes my pulse
            "Doc"

        shhh sshhhh

puts his finger on his lips

            too much yang
            hot & sweaty

need something cool

must eat the herbal soup laced with ginseng
a soufflé of beaten egg white

scallops in a shredded potato peel nest
or grilled sauté   of frog legs

a platter of black mushrooms
with snow peas

a bowl of chilly menthol jelly

light dessert
a pre/script/ion for hot damp weather

Singapore can surprise the hungry
melting
        mysteries

drug traders & pirates
preying upon local people
& foreigners
like Somerset Maugham
who searched among the opium dens
to find inspiration

orchid displays
welcome plant lovers & tree huggers

instead of an all night bar
you can visit the zoo

a midnight safari
full of jungle animals
roaming free in their habitat

maybe you'll feel at home
if you're searching for your muse

fireweed

by the lamppost
a swarm of mosquitoes
a man stands alone
against the weather

in baggy suspenders
he ploughs the dirt
sows seeds for his wheat field

shades of fireweed
a pile of stones
the harvest he doesn't expect

shoves back his broad-rimmed hat
smokes a cigar
kicks bales of straw
& moves rolls of hay

she peers out of the house
cut flowers in a vase
butter   jam & strawberry jelly
on a square slice of bread

skipping over rocks
progress & nostalgia
roam around

cornflower blue cracks
mapping the soil
earth shakes
crumbles under his feet

hyenas

the boss yells

> *told you to clear the underbrush*
> wilderness waits
> in the shadow
>
> dig into the skin
> tree trunks grow rough
> in the forest

workers sweat
toiling from dawn to dusk

black flies bite into flesh

African killer bees
swarm the swamps

you can drink tea
    to beat the heat

the hyenas cry in the distance
when night darkens the sky

my father says

> *they're hungry*
> *enough to lick*
> *cups & dishes clean*

with the foreman
he listens
to the forest dreaming of rain
smells of wet leaves & wild flowers

the cook prepares chicken soup
pours it into earthenware bowls

bakes bread on an open fire

hyenas laugh
closer to the camp
they eat crumbs from the plates
left out of the tent to dry

in the morning
the boss wakes up in a bad mood

shakes two scorpions out of his boots

screams at his crew
to work out a way through the forest

must find the road
no one has ever travelled before

my father still thinks of Ethiopia
wishing he'd never left the forest
                    in the rain

on the rocks

combing main street for a hotel room

midnight people
gazing at the mist
blackening
the vision of Tunnel mountain

        NO VACANCY
        flashing blood-red
        a flag on a rooftop

white streamers of lights

illusions/delusions

the tourist season at full speed
catching up to us

ten girls screaming
at the mannequin

                wait!

looks like a *real life* man
dressed up in coat & tails
         for his wedding

        Mann — do you take Kim
        for your lawful wife
        in good or bad times
        in illness or in health?

he turns into someone's groom
no longer a-sex-u-al
soul/rock singer
playing his electric guitar

performing
outside the stone Baptist church
where the choir
of voices
                    rises higher
to a rocky heaven

                    it's him
tugging at her creamy veil
folding it over

uncovers her face
showing the truth

innocence   is her name

he grins
but doesn't want champagne

takes off his top hat
digs into the black cylinder
for a surprise ending

free
a white-breasted dove
stretches its wings

candid admission to heaven
        faithfulness
        sincerity
        flying
out of his hat

a Pompei pilgrimage

to visit
the brick walls
encircling the terror of night?

a couple petrified in a dead city
in a code of silence

a bronze faun
dancing over the hot tiles of the atrium
witness to a different era of love

a girl alone in her bed
her dream trapped by molten lava
an abandoned nightmare
biting into raw stone

the baker's millstone & oven
by the open market

a house with an ancient fountain
& a cupid carrying a dolphin

on the western side of the Forum
Apollo is soaking up the sun
between ribbed columns
& a lone mosaic
showing how life used to be

a setter lies unmoving
as a hairy welcome rug
across a wide doorway

doesn't pant or wag its tail
a few buzzing flies circle the dog's head

        is the dog alive
        or just playing dead?
        the spotted caramel hair is matted
        soaked in sweat

i go closer
the setter doesn't budge

        is this dog sick?
        a heat stroke?
        a homeless stray with rabies?
        doesn't bark
        has bony legs
        don't know if the dog's still breathing
                needs the best care ever

i'd take the dog home with me
but it's too hot to worry

security stomps in
flashing a shiny silver badge

she pushes past me

        takes some notes

        picks up her cell phone
        & punches the right numbers

to get rid of a stray dog
whining for water

in brown laced-up boots

the hunk
takes his horse down
            to the creek at dawn

a Stetson hat on his head
backpack dangling

he cups his hands
drinks the fast-running water

hops over rust-coloured stones
to cross the stream
eroding the canyon

whirlpool   danger

pulling him down
forked branch clasps his boot laces tight

it's up to him to climb the steep slope
that leads to the top

the horse shakes its mane
& neighs
its tail whips the rancher's face

boots squish
dripping water
everything's going his way today

peppermint night

to Athanasius Kircher's
"Tower of Babel", *1679*

keeping a journal
                 a taste of things to come
solutions
to people's thirst for knowledge
                braiding a lattice of love

discovering friendship
desire
not just a presence
pine trees sculpting   pewter texture
             profile of the Rockies
daring you to try out your hand
among faces telling more than a story

scent of menthol
peppermint oil
spreading substance   new fads
who's *gonna* make it

if you drink this brew
you'll find the essence   of being
who we are   our selves
not anybody else
mint   & eucalyptus etching
       your breath
against night

spikes of language
                shoots of bluegrass
stick out of the cracks of the earth's belly

to find T-cells
                antibodies
crucial to the immune system
sounding the alarm to impulses

in the darkness   sparks
splicing   signals of fireflies
sending out messages   to you

conscience
an unknown idiom to the mind/flesh
in various codes

your ego
strikes your image with a hammer

> *"Chase the silhouette of the past*
> *Your dream's catching up*
> *Act out your feelings"*

flag down   dimensions
levels of meaning
fluidity
showing you
how you can feel/change

Vanna Tessier writes poetry dealing with the environment. We must face the world we live in today and we can accept reality as is. Either we take responsibility for our actions, or find refuge within the realm of imagery and fantasy.

A Selection of Our Titles in Print

A Fredericton Alphabet (John Leroux) photos, architecture	1-896647-77-4	$14.95
Avoidance Tactics (Sky Gilbert) drama	1-896647-50-2	15.88
Bathory (Moynan King) drama	1-896647-36-7	14.95
Combustible Light (Matt Santateresa) poetry	0-921411-97-9	12.95
Crossroads Cant (Mary Elizabeth Grace, Mark Seabrook, Shafiq, Ann Shin.		
Joe Blades, editor) poetry	0-921411-48-0	13.95
Cuerpo amado/Beloved Body (Nela Rio; Hugh Hazelton, translator)		
poetry	1-896647-81-2	15.88
Dark Seasons (Georg Trakl; Robin Skelton, trans.) poetry	0-921411-22-7	10.95
Day of the Dog-tooth Violets (Christina Kilbourne) novel	1-896647-44-8	17.76
for a cappuccino on Bloor (kath macLean) poetry	0-921411-74-X	13.95
Great Lakes logia (Joe Blades, ed.) art & writing anthology	1-896647-70-7	16.82
Heart-Beat of Healing (Denise DeMoura) poetry	0-921411-24-3	4.95
Heaven of Small Moments (Allan Cooper) poetry	0-921411-79-0	12.95
Herbarium of Souls (Vladimir Tasic) short fiction	0-921411-72-3	14.95
I Hope It Don't Rain Tonight (Phillip Igloliorti) poetry	0-921411-57-X	11.95
Jive Talk: George Fetherling in Interviews and Documents		
(George Fetherling; editor Joe Blades)	1-896647-54-5	13.95
Manitoba highway map (rob mclennan) poetry	0-921411-89-8	13.95
Notes on drowning (rob mclennan) poetry	0-921411-75-8	13.95
Railway Station (karl wendt) poetry	0-921411-82-0	11.95
Reader Be Thou Also Ready (Robert James) novel	1-896647-26-X	18.69
Rum River (Raymond Fraser) fiction	0-921411-61-8	16.95
Shadowy Technicians: New Ottawa Poets (ed. rob mclennan)		
poetry	0-921411-71-5	16.95
Song of the Vulgar Starling (Eric Miller) poetry	0-921411-93-6	14.95
Speaking Through Jagged Rock (Connie Fife) poetry	0-921411-99-5	12.95
Starting from Promise (Lorne Dufour) poetry	1-896647-52-9	13.95
Tales for an Urban Sky (Alice Major) poetry	1-896647-11-1	13.95
The Longest Winter (Julie Doiron, Ian Roy) photos, fiction	0-921411-95-2	18.69
These Are My Elders (Chad Norman; Heather Spears, ill.)	1-896647-74-X	13.95
The Sweet Smell of Mother's Milk-Wet Bodice		
(Uma Parameswaran) fiction	1-896647-72-3	13.95
Túnel de proa verde / Tunnel of the Green Prow (Nela Rio;		
Hugh Hazelton, translator) poetry	0-921411-80-4	13.95
What Was Always Hers (Uma Parameswaran) fiction	1-896647-12-X	17.95

www.brokenjaw.com hosts our current catalogue, submissions guidelines, manuscript award competitions, booktrade sales representation and distribution information. Broken Jaw Press eBooks of selected titles are available from http://www.PublishingOnline.com. Directly from us, all individual orders must be prepaid. All Canadian orders must add 7% GST/HST (Canada Customs and Revenue Agency Number: 12489 7943 RT0001).

BROKEN JAW PRESS, Box 596 Stn A, Fredericton NB E3B 5A6, Canada